Featherstone

Series editor
ALISTAIR BRYCE-CLEGG

50 fantastic ideas for fearless play

JUDIT HORVATH

Featherstone
An imprint of Bloomsbury Publishing Plc

50 Bedford Square
London
WC1B 3DP
UK

1385 Broadway
New York
NY 10018
USA

www.bloomsbury.com

Bloomsbury is a registered trademark of Bloomsbury Publishing Plc

First published 2017

British Library Cataloguing-in-Publication Data
A catalogue record for this book is available from the British Library.

ISBN:
PB 978-1-4729-4056-8
ePDF 978-1-4729-4057-5

Library of Congress Cataloging-in-Publication Data
A catalogue record for this book is available from the Library of Congress.

10 9 8 7 6 5 4 3 2 1

Printed and bound in India by Replika Press Pvt. Ltd.

Contents

Introduction

The main aim of the book

Whilst all children should be provided with a safe environment to play in, carers must always remember that risk-taking is a very important part of a child's healthy development. Denying opportunities to take risks and make decisions will negatively influence the children's abilities to grow responsibly and to lead happy lives. Risk, when linked to the care and protection of young children, generally raises many concerns, often leading to all perceived dangers being removed in the process of risk assessment. Unfortunately, parents and practitioners usually chose to err on the side of caution, as they're not comfortable differentiating between putting a child at risk, and allowing a child to take risks.

The main aim of the book is to provide ideas on how to approach risk within early years activities together with the children, on how to educate children about danger and on how to allow children to take risks that are necessary for them to develop thinking, problem-solving and decision-making abilities.

The structure of the book

The structure of the book is based on ideas for both indoor and outdoor risk-taking activities that will fit different types and levels of curriculum, providing a varied selection to suit different ages, stages and interests. Slightly differently from other books in the series, each of the activity subtitles highlights the risky element of the activity, so practitioners can decide in advance whether the activity would be suitable for the child/children they work with. Each activity description contains the list of resources required, titled 'What you need'. The activities are clearly explained step by step, with easy-to-follow instructions under the section 'What to do' with suggested extensions and variations for ensuring flexible provision to fit settings, children and individual needs. Additional ideas for similar activities prove very helpful when there is an instant need to take the learning further or to change the direction of the activity to keep the children's interest. The activity descriptions also highlight some observation questions that offer brief suggestions on how to follow the children's learning effectively, to enrich their learning in the future. For some activities adults need to accomplish certain tasks with additional care, demonstrating each step for children if they are to be completed safely. Practitioners should make informed decisions about which tasks can be safely accomplished by which of their children, and adhering to the Health & safety procedures in place within the childcare settings, every activity suggested in this book should be covered.
The section titled 'What's in it for the children?' describes the educational aims and learning opportunities of the activity.

What does 'fearless' mean in play?

Fearless play does not mean play with the absence of fear. Fearless play behaviour still includes asking questions, having doubts and being afraid. Fearless play is trying, acting, doing and completing tasks in spite of the things that children might find a little scary, with the faith that circumstances will work out and the benefit will be greater than the effort. Fearless is having the courage to allow oneself to try and fail and still feel proud. Accommodating and encouraging fearless play does not mean training the children to lose their sense of fear, instead it means teaching the children to overcome fear in order to achieve what they truly want.

Learning through the freedom of play

Young children are natural risk takers; they need and want to take risks. Taking acceptable risks will aid children when exploring personal limits, trying themselves in new skills and encountering unknown situations. Without taking risks or being strongly motivated to respond to challenges, children would never learn to crawl, kick a ball or ride a scooter. Play and risk are inseparable companions. True appreciation of children's play inevitably includes valuing risks.

As much as being natural risk takers, healthy children also have a natural ability to look after themselves to the point of their capabilities; however, they are not always able to understand their own limitations or assess the limitations of the environment they are in. Children, therefore, need confident adults around them who are fearless to some extent, in the sense of being unafraid to take risks and provide experiences with a safe level of risk, so they can – by imitating and listening – grow and develop skills to make choices about what they can safely attempt and what they cannot.

This book offers activities that will help practitioners provide well-managed opportunities for appropriate risk-taking to take place. Children nowadays have many things readily done for them, often only because it proves to be quicker, safer and easier for people taking care of them. For these children, having the opportunity to take risks is even more vital, as they may not always have the freedom of choice that they mentally and developmentally need. When completing the activities listed in this book, the sense of pride and achievement can motivate the children to reach their highest potential.

Lighting fire

Risk element: handling fire

What you need:

- Tape measure
- Rocks or stones for the fire circle
- Buckets of water or damp soil or sand
- A large collection of different sized logs, twigs and wood pieces
- Straw, leaves and bark
- Recycled paper
- Matchsticks

Taking it forward

- Children can make popcorn and toast, using a simple tool made by fixing two metal sieves together on a stick.
- Children can create a campfire in the dark and tell spooky stories.

What's in it for the children?

Children will enjoy each other's company, co-operation and working in a team. They will also exercise and learn about basic mathematical concepts regarding size comparison and shapes, and simple construction.

Observation questions

- How carefully does the child listen to instruction?
- Can the child understand basic concepts?

Health & Safety

Always make sure you have a means to extinguish fire. A bucket filled with damp sand or damp soil is ideal, as pouring water on a fire can cause it to spit, increasing the risk of burning.

What to do:

1. To prepare the area: situate the fire on a flat area, preferably dug about 5cm into the ground, at least 3 metres away from tents, trees, roots, overhanging boughs or dry leaves, and other flammable items. Clear a space 70 to 85cm across. Make a ring of rocks to contain the fire.
2. Make a fire control plan. Fill buckets with water or damp soil or sand, and have these on standby in case you need to put out the fire.
3. Gather firewood and kindling using only fallen branches as dry as possible. Divide them into three categories: thin ones (four of them together should be no thicker than a little finger), sticks about the thickness of a thumb, and about wrist-sized pieces. These categories pertain to stages of the fire.
4. Gather up a dense handful of pine straw, leaves, bark pieces or any other similar plant remains for starter fuel, such as paper or large leaves. Try ripping them into strips as thin as possible before lighting.
5. Build a small, loose pile of kindling in the fire circle, making sure to allow space for air to feed the fire. Include the paper scraps, dry plant matter, any type of wood shavings or straw and other small, flammable items.
6. Make an inward pointing tepee of dry twigs and small sticks around and above the kindling pile, leaving a gap on the side for entering air.
7. Light the kindling with a match.
8. Add increasingly larger sticks and then logs as the fire grows in strength, always leaving enough space between them for the fire to breathe, for example criss-cross the handfuls of twigs so that the fire can get air. Place your largest sticks in an arrangement that gives them stability and exposure to the fire without suppressing the airflow to the heart of the fire.
9. When the fire is done, take special care to completely, exhaustively extinguish every last ember.

ıaking kindling

isk element: handling a knife

What you need:

- Safety gloves
- A large collection of different sized twigs and wood pieces
- Bushcraft knives (sharp, undamaged ones) alternatively a hand axe
- As a variation, thicker sticks and good quality potato peelers

What to do:

1. To prepare the area: situate the children at least arm's length from each other, sitting steadily with no objects around.
2. Demonstrate the activity in a clearly visible area.
3. Make sure the children wear strong safety gloves, or at least that they wear one on their non-working hand.
4. For older children, show them how to swing a hand axe at a small piece of wood that is held by hand to make kindling.
5. A safer technique, or for younger children, is to hold the piece of wood to be split in place on a chopping block with a 'sissy stick' – that is a stick just long enough to get the steadying hand out of the way of the hand axe.
6. Hold the axe near the head so that you are using the axe's weight, not its speed, to split the wood.
7. The same method can be tried with sharp bushcraft knives. Hold a longer piece of wood steadily with one hand on your legs, so the end of the wood is in the air, not on your legs. With the other hand carve the wood away from the body.
8. Alternatively, younger children can use potato peelers to carve thicker sticks.

aking it forward

- Children can collect different types and sized fir cones as kindling, which can also act as an identifying activity. Depending on age, children can go in pairs or alone (without adult supervision), but the exact boundaries have to be agreed prior to their collecting walk.
- Children can create tightly rolled newspaper sticks, using scissors to cut and raffia pieces to tie

Vhat's in it for the children?

:hildren will learn about personal ;pace, that of their own and others, so hey will understand basic safety rules vhen handling potentially dangerous ›bjects. They will practise following ;tep-by-step instructions.

)bservation questions

- Can children demonstrate strengths to handle larger tools?
- Do children show an awareness of space of their own and that of others, and understand basic safety measures?

Marshmallow toasting

Risk element: handling a knife, handling fire

What you need:

- A large collection of different sized twigs and wood pieces
- Bucket filled with water or damp sand or soil
- Recycled paper
- Dry tinder such as paper, grass, dryer lint, char cloth or small twigs
- Matchsticks
- Marshmallows

Taking it forward

- Organise a cooking/recipe competition that will use toasted marshmallows. Make smores, biscuit icing, toasted strawberry shortcakes, marshmallow and peanut butter sandwiches etc.
- Encourage children to prepare a pictorial marshmallow-toasting guide using their own photos and drawings.
- Older children can make their own bucket fire (in purpose-made buckets).

What's in it for the children?

When enjoyed together, children can experience a real sense of community, sharing and love with this activity. The togetherness usually sparks communication and therefore encourages natural, personal storytelling. Being in a group can aid shy children to overcome their worries and barriers.

Observation questions

- Can children demonstrate an understanding of cause and effect (to further aid the knowledge of basic safety)?
- Do children approach new situations (like the fire) with confidence?

What to do:

1. To prepare: build a fire in a large clear area, preferably lowered by being dug slightly in the ground. Ideally, start this an hour in advance so you have time to get logs that are perfect roasting fuel. Make sure you have fire buckets nearby.
2. Use a pile of dry tinder, such as paper, grass, dryer lint, char cloth or small twigs which work well as kindling, then gradually, once the fire catches, add dry branches about the size of your forearm.
3. Choose the roasting sticks from your wood pieces: hardwood sticks, sap-free and whittled to a blunt point.
4. Poke a marshmallow onto a stick. Make sure the stick goes all the way through the marshmallow to prevent slipping. Work with one at a time to achieve a good toasted surface.
5. Roast the marshmallow over the burning logs. Once your fire has been burning for a while, some of the wood will burn out and turn into glowing 'coals'. A spot right above these coals is the perfect area to roast marshmallows. (Expect charcoal if marshmallows are put directly in the fire.)
6. Turn gradually. Rotate the stick, so the heat toasts the marshmallow evenly all the way round.
7. Take care not to accidentally hold marshmallows above a flame. Unlike the coals, which just radiate heat, the flames also send a stream of hot gases travelling upward so it can end up turning the marshmallows black or even setting it on fire.

ypsy flowers

isk element: handling sharp equipment

OUTDOOR PLAY

What you need:

- Safety gloves
- A large collection of different sized twigs and rods, as straight as possible
- Small saw
- Hand drill
- Vice and workbench if possible
- Draw knives (sharp, undamaged ones)
- Alternatively, potato peelers

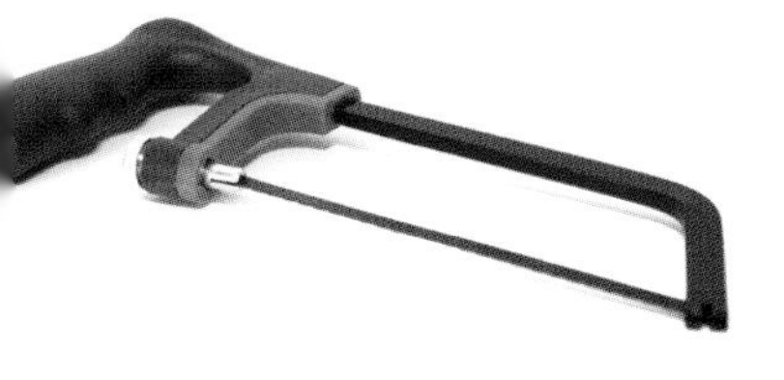

What to do:

1. To prepare the area: situate the children at least an arm's length from each other, sitting steadily with no objects around them.
2. Demonstrate the activity in a clearly visible area.
3. Make sure the children wear a strong safety glove on their non-working hand.
4. Use a saw to cut a rod into a length of half a metre or so.
5. Use a hand drill to form a hole at one end of the rod, approx 1.5cm deep.
6. Keeping the drilled hole end of the rod pointed towards you, grip it in a vice and begin to shave the bark off, moving the knife or potato peeler towards you, stopping at the end of the rod.
7. Keep turning the rod as you shave, allowing the rod to become thinner and eventually break off.
8. Insert a stick into the hole to make a realistic flower on a stem.

king it forward

For variety, add willow branches to make a flower bush.

Create a bouquet from different style flowers, made out of different types of twigs.

hat's in it for the children?

ildren will learn about the materials their environment whilst also having a ance to express their artistic thoughts an unusual medium away from a assroom.

servation questions

Do the children show an interest in different types of media?

Do children express their own views via art?

Bow and arrow making

Risk element: handling sharp equipment

What you need:

- **Small handsaw for cutting branches**
- **Long branches and sticks that can be readily cut**
- **Knives** (sharp, undamaged ones)
- **String**
- **Tape measure**
- **Stone or other blunt object, for arrowhead**
- **Duct tape**
- **Feather**
- **Glue** (optional)

What to do:

1. Find the freshest wood possible – ideally cut a branch directly off a tree, but wood can be sourced elsewhere as well. To make the bow the ideal branch would be flexible, snap right back into place when bent and also have a slight natural curve. Arrows require special woo Find a stick that is thin, lightweight, and strong. This wi help ensure that the arrow flies fast and straight.
2. Clean the branches and sticks. Remove all extra twigs and the bark in order to make the bow easier to hold ar the arrow easier to release.
3. Cut string ready to use, 15cm shorter than the bow itse to ensure the bow has tension and curve after it has been strung. Thinner, stronger string is best.
4. Make two slits on the bow stick. These should be abou 2cm from each end of the branch.
5. Anchor the string by tying a strong knot at one of the slits. Pull on the string to make sure it stays in place.
7. String the bow. Bend the bow and slowly pull the knot until it reaches the slit on the other end of the bow. The string should be tied tight to give the bow a slight curv but has to be unstringable, as when you've finished practising if it's left strung for too long the bow will ben and lose tension.

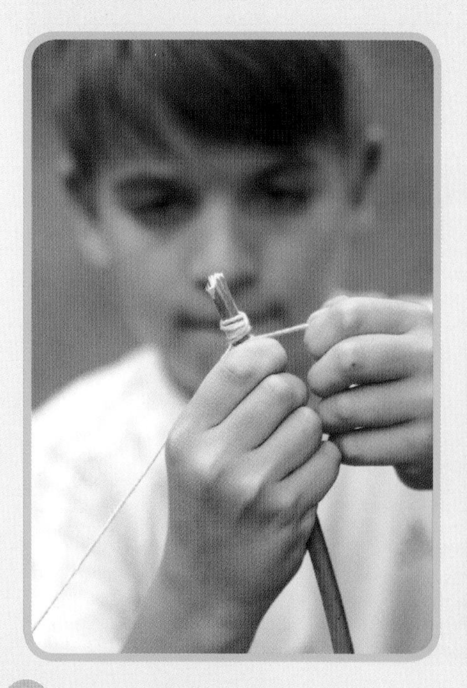

- To make the arrow attach the arrowhead to your strong, thin stick. Use a stone or other small, blunt object and attach it to the end of arrow with duct tape, or wrap the entire end of the arrow in duct tape to reduce damage caused by impact.
- Attach the fletching, the material at the end of the arrow which helps guide it as it flies. Find some feathers and glue them onto the back ends of the arrows or split the back of the arrow, slide the feather in, and tightly wrap a thin thread around the fletching.
- Nock the arrow. Take a knife and cut a slit at the end without the arrowhead to make the nock. This will help the string guide the arrow.

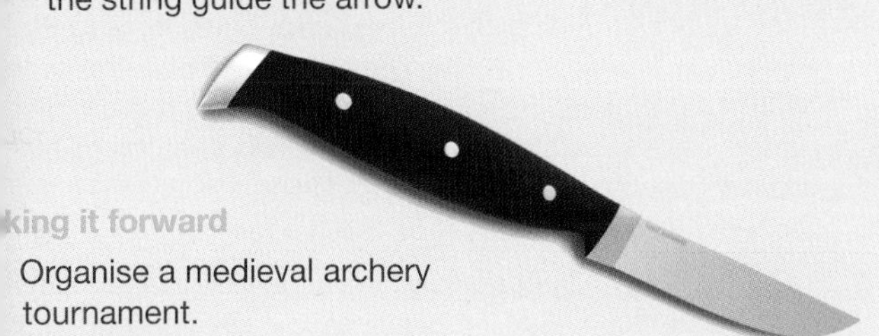

king it forward

- Organise a medieval archery tournament.
- Set simple challenges for the children to earn their 'archery licence'.

hat's in it for the children?

ildren will learn about how natural aterials have been used for different rposes in different times of human story. They will gain a simple derstanding of how to minimise risk d how to take acceptable risks with fety in mind.

servation questions

- Do the children show interest in taking risks?
- Do children approach risk in an acceptable way (showing awareness, being able to overcome fears, showing a caring attitude towards self and others)?

Health & Safety

Remind the children never to point the arrows at each other, and to take care not to poke themselves in the eye when positioning the arrow or drawing the bow.

Rope ladder

Risk element: handling tools and sharp equipment

What you need:

- Tape measure
- Wood dowels or wood pieces
- Chopsaw/tablesaw
- Paracord
- Masking tape

Taking it forward

- Study different types of 'ladders' used by animals in nature. Discuss the risks they take.

What's in it for the children?

Children will learn about how natural materials can be used for different purposes and how they can support themselves with self-made items. They will gain confidence and courage and as the completion of the project needs teamwork, they will also learn about working together.

Observation questions

- Do the children show understanding of the physical limits of the human body?
- Do children help each other?
- Do they follow instructions in a sequence?

What to do:

1. To check how much rope you need, decide how tall the ladder should be. Take the desired height, multiply by tw and add extra for the knots.
2. Rungs need to be about 20cm wide to be strong enoug These can be made from purchased dowel or foraged wood.
3. Cut the rungs from the dowel /foraged wood using a chopsaw or tablesaw.
4. Make a very narrow U-shape from the paracord. Take a piece of masking tape and mark the centre of the U.
5. Use a tight and economic constrictor knot: moving the paracord from right to left, wrap it around one end of th dowel rung twice. Feed the longer end of the paracord under the two wraps to secure it. Pull both ends of the cord to tighten the knot. Try practising this knot a coupl of times before you use it on the ladder.
6. Try to get the two pieces of paracord going to the first rung the same length. This will help keep your ladder balanced. Use the constrictor knot to tie the paracord around the rungs at each end. Try to get the spacing on either side of the rung roughly the same. This is where the tape measure will be useful.
7. Now, just repeat this step until completed. Keep spacin in mind, try to make it all equal.
8. When complete, make sure all of the knots are tightene and properly aligned so they won't slide.
9. There are many ways the ladder can be mounted. Test the ladder very carefully close to the surface before letting the children use it. Then also test the natural tree branch that you have chosen to mount it on.
10. For smaller children mount the ladder on a shallow hill f simple but challenging fun.

Foraging

isk element: possibility of getting poked, scratched or stung

What you need:

- Waterproof clothing for children
- Small knives
- Small baskets/trugs/plastic bags
- Hand towels
- Water bottles
- Field guides to edible plants

king it forward

Cook or bake with the children's own foraged ingredients, such as herb biscuits, berry pudding etc.

Make children's own foraging maps.

hat's in it for the children?

ildren will be excited about collecting d making things from the natural eas nearby and they will enjoy this cus on edible plants. The activity lps children to better understand the rth, learning about habitat, wildlife, eather, microclimates, soil, and ore. Foraging anchors children in the asons, enabling them to become ndful of the here and now.

servation questions

Does the child show an interest in their environment?

Does the child compare different places in their life (home/nursery/ nanny's house etc.)?

Health & Safety

Make it clear that the children may only eat plants that you and they are confident are safe.

What to do:

1. Look for field guides to edible plants at your local library.
2. Connect with an advanced wild food enthusiast. Find a foraging mentor through your local nature centre.
3. Discover a few favourite foraging sites nearby.
4. Check with the local park office or land owners to determine if foraging is allowed on their property.
5. Discuss the possible risks with children before the trip and create a pictorial guide about how to approach risk, including ditches, natural water, falling branches, unknown plants, animals etc.
6. Forage plants that are easy to pick and hard to confuse with anything else, such as berries (blackberries, raspberries, strawberries, elderberries), nettles, dandelions, rosemary, lavender, damson, or watercress.

Nettle soup

Risk element: possibility of getting stung, handling hot appliances

What you need:

- Field guides
- Long-sleeved tops and long trousers for children
- Rubber or plastic gloves
- Supermarket bags
- Large trays
- Cooking implements:
  - large saucepans
  - wooden spoon
  - blender
- Soup ingredients:
  - 1 onion, chopped
  - 1 tbsp oil
  - 2 garlic cloves, chopped
  - 250g nettle leaves, washed
  - 1 litre water
  - 1 tsp vegetable bouillon powder
  - 1 tbsp uncooked pudding rice
  - 250g new potatoes, diced
  - salt and black pepper, optional
  - yoghurt

What's in it for the children?

Children will be excited about collecting nettles and making food from them. The activity will help children to better understand the natural world and the part they play in it, which in turn will encourage them to take healthy risks.

Observation questions

- Do the children use their previous knowledge when approaching risks?
- Do the children show empathy/help each other in case of getting hurt?

What to do:

1. Find a local park where you can pick nettles.
2. Nettles are best when very tender, so pick them in the spring when they are just coming up or near the end of the season.
3. Pick the young leaves from the tips of the nettle stems.
4. Use rubber gloves, or you could even pick them bare-handed, pinching the leaves hard to avoid getting stung
5. Once picked, lay the nettles out on a tray to wilt.
6. Once wilted they can no longer sting. (The sting relies o erect hairs to penetrate the skin and inject the stinging formic acid.) Strip the leaves off the stems.
7. When cooked, nettles reduce to about a quarter of the amount.
8. To make the soup: in a large saucepan, sauté the onion in the oil until soft. Add the garlic and quickly stir-fry. Ac the nettles, 700 ml of water and the vegetable bouillon powder. Simmer gently for 30 minutes. In another saucepan add 300 ml of water, rice and diced potato and cook until the rice and potato are tender. Take off the heat. Blend the nettle mixture until smooth. In a larg saucepan mix the blended nettle with the rice and the potato mix and heat through. Season to taste and add black pepper and a swirl of yoghurt.

Taking it forward

- Make nettle tea: pick and wash nettles, then dry them on a large, clean kitchen towel for several days, until completely dry and brittle.
- Make nettle lotion: pick nettles and rinse them in water. Crush them in a pestle and mortar together with fresh lavender until mushy and add to a base cream made of equal parts of coconut oil and petroleum jelly.

Pond dipping

Risk element: handling live animals, playing around deep water

What you need:

- Nets with long handles
- Plastic pots and trays
- Plastic spoons
- Magnifying glasses
- Pond-life identification guides

What to do:

1. Find a local pond that is accessible with a group of children. Ask for advice from the Local Authority.
2. Plan the trip and allow enough time for good observation.
3. To carry out the dipping: just sweep the nets slowly through the water, trying to avoid stirring up the bottom too much. Going over the same area a few times can often be a good approach, because it tends to catch things which have been disturbed as they try to make their getaway.
4. Transfer the animals you catch to a pot or container that's been filled with pond water. An identification guide is indispensable – even if you're an expert on pond-life yourself – to allow the children to identify their catch.

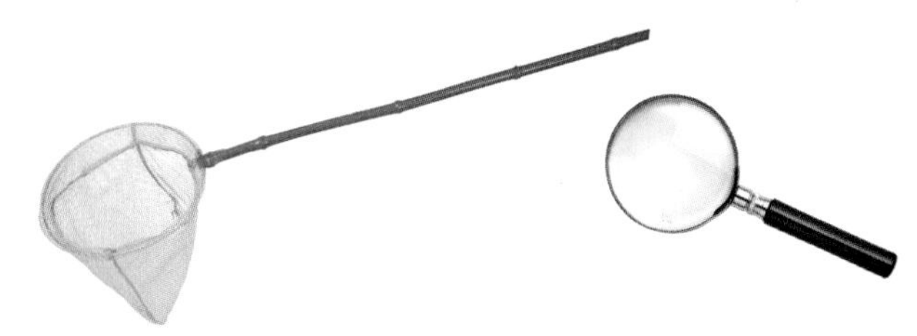

Taking it forward

- Visit a larger lake or river further away as a part of the day trip.
- Compile a pictorial water identification guide and invite a small parent group to visit with children as tour guides.

What's in it for the children?

Children will gain a general picture of their local living space. Pond dipping anchors children in their environment and helps them to look after all living beings.

Observation questions

- Does the child show interest in all parts of their environment?
- Does the child compare different places in their life (home/nursery/nanny's house etc.)?

Health & Safety

Discuss the safety rules with the children in advance: how to be careful around the edge of the water (no running, pushing or general fooling around) how to keep out of the water, how to avoid putting anything from the pond (or that's been dipped into the pond) into their mouths, and how to use eyes for observation, avoiding touching (some kinds of pond-life can give nips).

Fishing

Risk element: handling sharp equipment

What you need:

- A strong piece of stick, as straight as possible
- Knife
- Fishing line or strong, thin thread
- Large fishing hooks
- Large fresh breadcrumbs for bait
- Safety gloves

Taking it forward

- Clean and cook the fish over an open fire, if the catch is a species that is good to eat.
- Photograph the children's catch and prepare an identification guide.
- Use large, wader-like wellington boots so you can fish standing in the water.

What's in it for the children?

Children can experience providing basic ingredients for themselves in natural surroundings and this focus will develop the children's interest and therefore their knowledge.

Observational questions

- Does the child concentrate on longer, more complex tasks?
- Can the child identify different fish and do they express an interest in this?

Health & Safety

- When making the fishing pole, wear a safety glove on the non-working hand.
- Making the fishing line and hook is delicate work and won't be possible with safety gloves on. Make sure children take especial care with the sharp hook.

What to do:

1. Find a local pond that is accessible with a group of children. Ask for advice from the Local Authority.
2. Plan the trip and allow enough time for setting up the fishing tackle (for example, cut the stick for the fishing rod in the local environment together with the children).
3. Discuss the safety rules with the children in advance such as how to be careful around the edge of the water (no running, pushing or general fooling around), how to keep out of the water, how to avoid putting anything from the pond (or that's been dipped into the pond) into their mouths. Demonstrate how to cut with the knife away from the body.
4. To make the fishing pole: find a living tree branch 2 to 3m long and about the diameter of an adult thumb. Cut off the desired length. Cut away shoots, side branches and leaves to achieve a tapering pole. Test the tip of the fishing rod by bending it with your hand.
5. To make the fishing line: Use fishing line or sewing thread to string the pole, or for a more natural end product green vines in the undergrowth around bushes or tangled in ground cover can also be used. Tie the line about midway down the pole and wrap it three to four times along the length of the pole toward the tip. Tie the line around the tip of the fishing pole to hold it securely for casting. Tie your hook on at the bottom of the dangling end of the line. You could purchase hooks to bring with you, or carve your own from a stick.
6. Turn over rocks around moss and in moist, shaded areas to find earthworms for bait. Grubs and crickets or pieces of bread can also be used. Bait the hook and gently swing the line into the water, targeting still pools, eddies and areas behind exposed boulders in a river. Bank fishing right near the water's edge will also produce fish.
7. Allow the children to identify their catch.

Basket making

Risk element: handling sharp tools

What you need:

- Brown paper
- Ruler
- Pencil
- Scissors
- Bendy stick
- Stapler
- Glue
- Raffia

What to do:

1. Cut brown paper into two squares measuring 15 cm by 15 cm. Place the pieces of paper on top of each other. The paper on the top will become the lining of the basket, whilst the paper on the bottom will become the outside of the basket.
2. Use a ruler to draw a grid onto the top sheet to make nine even squares.
3. With both sheets of paper held together, fold the paper into thirds (following the grid lines). Repeat to ensure a crisp fold on all grid edges.
4. Use scissors to cut two lines from two opposite edges in towards the centre square of the grid. The centre square of the grid will become the base of the basket.
5. Bring the edges in towards the centre to form the sides of the basket and staple into place. Repeat with the other sides of the basket.
6. Cut a small piece of bendy stick and staple it to the outsides of the box to form a handle.
7. Apply glue to the outer surface of the basket and roll raffia around the outer of the basket, starting from the bottom. This will help to achieve a woven basket look.

aking it forward

Help the children to use tools correctly by preparing a route towards acquiring a 'tool licence' that children earn by showing their understanding of basic safety rules.

Prepare a tool box with real tools and have nominated 'tool days'.

/hat's in it for the children?

hildren will learn how to use small and tools correctly. This will aid the evelopment of their fine motor skills, hilst also developing their confidence nd courage.

bservation questions

Does the child show understanding of how to handle sharp tools?

Does the child understand different tools and their uses?

Target making

Risk element: handling tools, handling sharp equipment, throwing heavy object

What you need:

- Workbench and vice
- Thin plywood
- Woodworking clamps
- Tape measure
- Pencil
- Small handsaw
- Safety glove
- Hand drill
- Different sized paper plates
- String
- Pebbles
- Paint

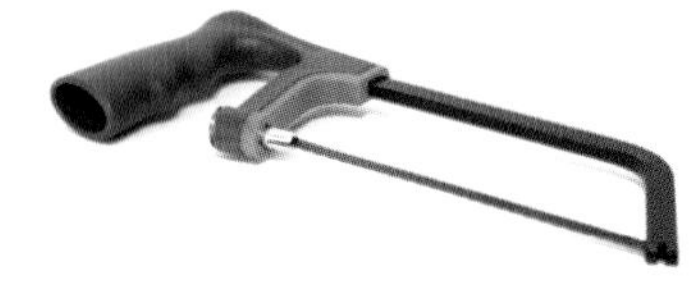

What to do:

1. Secure the wood to a workbench with a vice. Leave plenty of space to work around the wood. Attach woodworking clamps to the wood and the surface that the wood is resting on before beginning.
2. Make a square for the base as it is an easy shape for the children to cut. Use a tape measure to determine the size of the wood, and where it needs to be cut. With a pencil, mark the line to be cut.
3. Place the handsaw on top of the wood, slightly away from where the cut line was drawn (the saw doesn't cut along a one dimensional line, it cuts a path of about 1 to 2mm).
4. Angle the far edge of the handsaw down towards the ground, and slightly raise the elbow that is holding the saw.
5. Grip the handle of the saw. The grip should be firm but relaxed: demonstrate it for the children. The body should also be in a relaxed posture to avoid accidents.
6. The hand that is not holding the saw should rest on the piece of wood in order to keep it still and secure. Be sure to keep that hand a good distance from the saw to prevent an accident, and also make sure it is covered with a safety glove.

- Start the cut by pulling back the saw without applying any pressure. Once the saw has made a slight cut into the wood, check that children are cutting in the right direction and at the right angle.
- Start applying pressure. Lightly press down on the saw and keep cutting through the wood – the sawing motion should be smooth and accurate.
- Continue the sawing motion until the piece of wood is ready to break off. Slow down and apply less force towards the end, to avoid cracking or splintering the wood. Hold onto the piece that is about to be cut off to prevent the weight of the wood from breaking off in splinters.

0. Working in pairs, make holes on two corners of the wood with a hand-drill, so the target can be hung.

1. To create the target, use different sized paper plates and draw descending circles, placing the smaller circle in the middle of the bigger one. Encourage the children to be as accurate as possible. Make two even holes at the top of the target and thread though with string, then hang the target from the holes in the plywood base.

2. Stand a good distance from the target and take it in turns to aim and throw pebbles at the bull's-eye. For a competitive, fun element, apply paint to the pebbles, to mark the exact place of the shot.

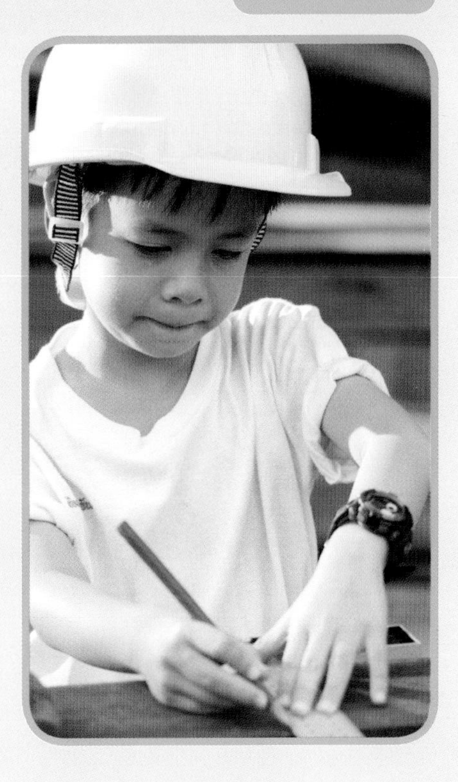

Taking it forward

- Organise a medieval knight tournament.
- Balloons filled with a little bit of baby powder create a smoke effect when shot.

What's in it for the children?

Children will learn about how natural materials have been used for different purposes in different times through human history. They will gain a simple understanding of how to minimise risk and how to take acceptable risks with safety in mind.

Observation questions

- Do the children show an interest in history and historical changes? Do they display an interest in the concept of time?
- Do children display a healthy, social attitude towards competition?

Berry picking

Risk element: possibility of getting scratched, poked or stung

What you need:

- Clothing that covers the children's skin: closed shoes, long trousers and long sleeves
- Small knives
- Small baskets/trugs/plastic bags

Taking it forward

- Make a hot blackberry sauce on the stove to eat with muffins.
- Use a blender to make a blackberry and banana smoothie.

What's in it for the children?

Children can gain a better understanding of the risk-benefit assessment, so they can make informed choices about approaching slightly risky activities without a fear of negative results, which will greatly support their confidence and self-esteem.

Observation questions

- Is the child able to overcome fear?
- Does the child use their body-control to avoid risk?

What to do:

1. Look for a local field with brambles.
2. Check with the land owners to determine if foraging is allowed on their property.
3. Discuss the possible risks with children before the trip and create a pictorial guide about how to approach risks connected to the bramble.
4. Wear closed shoes, long trousers, and long sleeves to protect the skin from stings and bites.
5. Gloves are also helpful but tend to snag on the thorns; so aid braver children in accepting a few scratched fingers as the small cost of the joy of picking berries.

_og walkway

isk element: handling heavy objects, playing on height

What you need:

- Large rocks
- Large logs and tree trunk pieces
- Wheelbarrow
- Shovel

What to do:

1. Collect a selection of large rocks, logs and trunk pieces, possibly with flat surfaces on each side.
2. Find a large area with a soft, relatively clean surface.
3. Discuss with the children how they imagine their walkway to appear (in a line, in a semi-circle or a zigzag etc.) and make a plan for how to move and organise the rocks and logs.
4. Discuss the possible risks with children before starting the project.
5. Move the larger pieces one by one with the wheelbarrow.
6. Dig small holes to support the rocks and logs so the children can stand and walk on them.
7. Arrange the pieces, and try the construction first before allowing children to use it.

aking it forward

- Time children when walking through the walkway in order to set their personal records.
- Try a variety of movements when walking on the walkway: arms out to the side, arms raised above their heads.

/hat's in it for the children?

hildren can challenge their own hysical boundaries and encourage iemselves to 'push their limits'. his activity will support their hysical development, their stamina, onfidence and self-esteem.

bservation questions

- Is the child able to understand physical boundaries?
- How does the child react to challenge?

Tepee building

Risk element: handling heavy objects, handling sharp tools

What you need:

- Four large logs, about equal lengths, at least as tall as the children but possibly taller
- Strong rope
- Matches
- A large sheet, tarpaulin or plastic sheeting
- Screws and washers
- Scissors
- Hand drill

What to do:

1. Collect a selection of large logs.
2. Cut a large length of rope and burn the end.
3. Drill holes in two of the logs at about 12-15cm.
4. Create a practice tepee with the poles to see how they need to lie to be stable. Using four logs for the poles, it's best to have the front wider and the back of the tepee narrower.
5. String rope through the holes and tie a knot where it meets the pole.
6. Feed the rope through the second pole, then wrap it around a couple of times in various directions to stabilise it.
7. Add the third pole, testing where to place it, drill the hole, feed the rope through and wrap.
8. Repeat for the fourth pole. Wrap the rope over and under, then around the tepee several times.
9. Open the sheet, tarpaulin or plastic sheeting horizontally and find the middle. Start draping it from the back of the tepee and secure it at the top of your tepee with one screw. Drill a hole through the pole and fabric, add a washer to the screw and insert the screw through both fabric and the pole.
10. Continue draping the fabric around the sides as it falls naturally, tucking under the excess on the floor, trying to keep it tight and uniform where the poles meet. Adjust your poles slightly if needed, then use a screw on each side to secure the fabric.
11. Roll or cut the excess fabric in the interior.

Taking it forward

- Create a campsite outdoors by making several tepees. Use a shovel to partially bury the tepee poles for prolonged use.

What's in it for the children?

Children can understand the basic rules of physical structures and balance, how objects stand and support weight. This will aid them in understanding how to approach physically risky activities in their environment.

Taking it forward

- Does the child show an interest in the basic rules of physics?
- Can the child connect themself to the environment?

Leaf play

Risk element: possibility of falling, environmental factors

What you need:

- A large area with a selection of fallen leaves or cut grass
- Bale of hay

Taking it forward

- Create funny structures by trying to cover children with fallen leaves.
- Try to copy the movements of falling leaves.

What's in it for the children?

Children can gain a sense of freedom and a sense of their own physical being. This aids them in respecting their body, their own space and that of others, which can naturally reduce the risk associated with physical activities.

Observation questions

- Does the child show respect for others?
- Can the child follow instructions whilst they are encouraged to act freely?

What to do:

1. Find an area with fallen leaves and cut grass. A small hillside location adds to the fun. Alternatively lay a small bale of hay on the surface.
2. Allow the children to freely move in the area, including running, kicking, throwing etc.
3. Encourage the children to look out for each other and respect each other's physical space and freedom as much as possible.
4. Discuss with the children what their body feels like before/during/after the activity.
5. Repeat the activity in several variations such as: try to cover one of their body parts or their friends in leaves, move following music or imitate animal movements.

Raft making

Risk element: handling sharp tools, playing around deep water

What you need:

- Knife
- Four sticks of equal length for the frame
- Eight to ten sticks of similar length to the frame to create the bed of the raft
- Strong thread or long grass stems
- A large leaf or a frond of leaves for the sail
- A stick for the mast

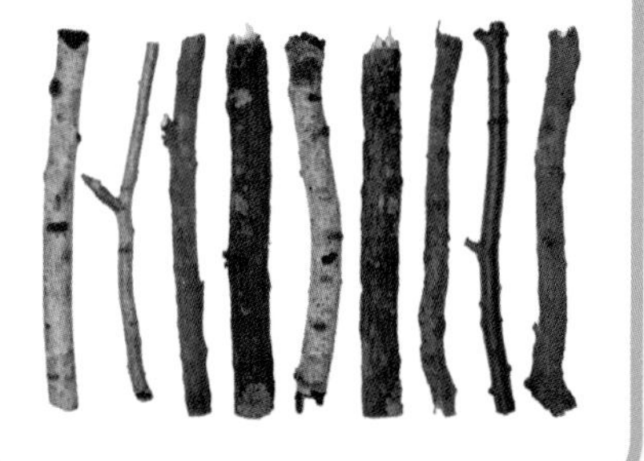

What to do:

1. Aid and encourage the children to cut the necessary branches to provide the required amount of sticks.
2. If you opt to make a frame: lay the four sticks for the frame on top of each other to estimate size. Carefully wind a thread or a long grass reed around each of the joints, overlapping and winding from one corner to the other. This will hold them in place. Complete for each corner.
3. Once the frame is completed, fix sticks to the frame to make the bed of the raft, winding the grass over in a cross style in between the sticks. Continue until the base is covered, or – if a frame is not used – until the desired size is achieved.
4. To give your raft a more stylish appearance, add a raft and sail. Use one stick as the mast and a large leaf as the sail. Make two small holes in the raft to push the mast through. Insert it into a gap in between two of the sticks, and carefully wrap grass around it to fix it into place.
5. Encourage the children to stand in the water and sail the raft, and test its strength by placing a variety of objects on top of it.

·king it forward

- Organise a raft sailing competition.
- Take children on a boat trip.

'hat's in it for the children?

hildren will gain knowledge of the ıaracteristics of water and connect · the natural water environment. This ill aid them in understanding the ys and the risks of playing in natural ıvironments, and also help them to ɔproach it without fear.

bservation questions

- Does the child show understanding of the theory of sinking/floating?
- Does the child understand the notion of depth?

Health & Safety

Always monitor children closely when near and around water, and make sure they know not to run around or splash each other, or put anything from or around the pond near their mouths.

Bush hide and seek

Risk element: possibility of getting scratched, poked or stung

What you need:

- An area with a variety of plants, small trees, bushes and long grass

What to do:

1. Find an area with a variety of plants, small trees, bushes and long grass.
2. Discuss the possible risks with the children, such as getting scratches or being poked by branches or fallen tree pieces, getting stung by nettles, tripping or falling. Urge the children to be vigilant.
3. Nominate a child from the group and ask them to blindfold themselves with their hands.
4. Encourage the other children to hide between the plants, trees, bushes etc.
5. Play the hide and seek variation Marco Polo, where the 'it' player of the tag shouts out Marco and the other players respond by saying Polo, so they can try to acoustically locate the others. You may need to explain that Marco Polo was a famous explorer!

Taking it forward

- Play 'number war': place a paper number plate on the children's foreheads, so the player who is 'it' has to identify the number on each of the other players' heads.
- Play 'blindfolded smell tag': on a large, open, grassy area without obstacles nominate an 'it' player, and place smelly items in the other players' hands, such as vinegar, flowers, perfume, air freshener etc.

What's in it for the children?

Children can gain deeper knowledge of their local environment with its joys and risks. It will help them to develop their confidence and self-esteem.

Observation questions

- Do the children follow rules and instructions?
- Do the children notice their environment?

·landling real tools

isk element: handling sharp tools, handling electric equipment

What you need:

- A selection of tools: screwdriver, hand drill, saw, electric screwdriver, hammer, electric mixer
- Safety gloves
- Safety glasses
- A selection of pieces of wood

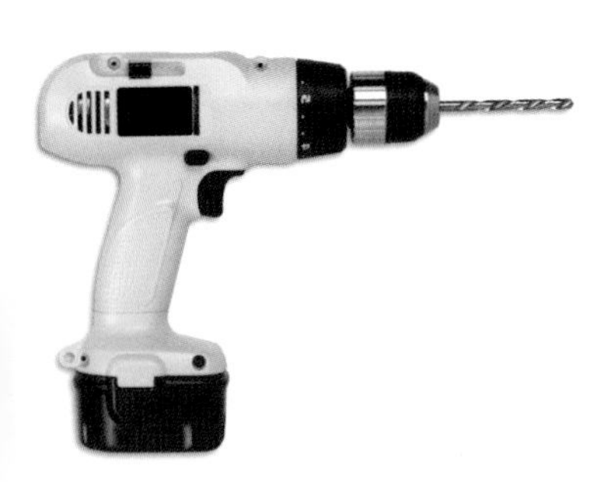

What to do:

1. Collect a selection of real tools and electric appliances for the children to try out, and gather a selection of pieces of wood for them to work with.
2. Discuss the risks related to each tool with the children.
3. Demonstrate the correct use of the tools one by one. Make sure that the children wear a safety glove on their non-working hand when doing this activity.
4. Set up different stations such as a drilling table, hammering table, mixing table etc. (depending on the selection of tools).
5. Divide the children into groups (allocate an adult helper to each group) and allow them to try handling the tools.
6. Take photos to look through later, discussing the experience with the children when you do so.

ıking it forward

Discuss the health and safety rules of tool handling and prepare a pictorial guide with the children.

Use the tools with purpose and prepare small items such as a birdhouse, reform an old chair into a shelf, etc.

/hat's in it for the children?

ɦildren will develop a sense of ɛsponsibility whilst also bettering ıeir physical skills and concentration. ɦey will connect themselves to the ɖult world and take a step towards ɦderstanding life responsibilities.

bservation questions

Does the child show a sense of responsibility?

Does the child show a basic understanding of risks?

Building a brick wall

Risk element: handling hot substance, handling heavy objects

What you need:

- Play concrete/plaster of Paris or playdough:
  - 2 cups of plain flour
  - ½ cup salt
  - 1½ cups of boiling water,
  - 2 tbsps oil and grey food colouring
- Small pieces of real brick, recycled from building sites
- Small dinner knife/spatula
- Small shovel and other small tools
- Optional: toy cars, construction hat, wooden road signs

What to do:

1. Find a large, clear area where the children can work undisturbed.
2. Prepare the playdough or plaster of Paris, which will be your 'concrete' with the children by mixing all the ingredients together.
3. Encourage the children to 'prebuild' the wall by arranging the bricks as they want them, without any 'concrete' yet, to see how it will look.
4. Encourage the children to build the wall, using the dinner knife or spatula to apply the 'concrete' between the bricks.
5. Leave the wall to set and use it in imaginative play scenarios.

Health & Safety

If you use plaster of Paris rather than playdough, remember not to pour the plaster or plaster water down the sink.

king it forward

- Encourage children to draw a design and then try to make it using blocks and playdough.
- Allow children to free play with the materials and then draw or write about their experience or what they constructed.
- Use as a starter activity for children's storytelling.
- Challenge children to copy well known building structures.

'hat's in it for the children?

nildren will develop concentration and erseverance as they build. They will ain an understanding of basic physical eories such as balance, gravity etc.

bservation questions

- Can the children express their impressions about the experience?
- Can the children notice small details?

Builder helpers

Risk element: handling sharp equipment

What you need:

- Old or unused wood with nails and screws in
- A selection of pliers

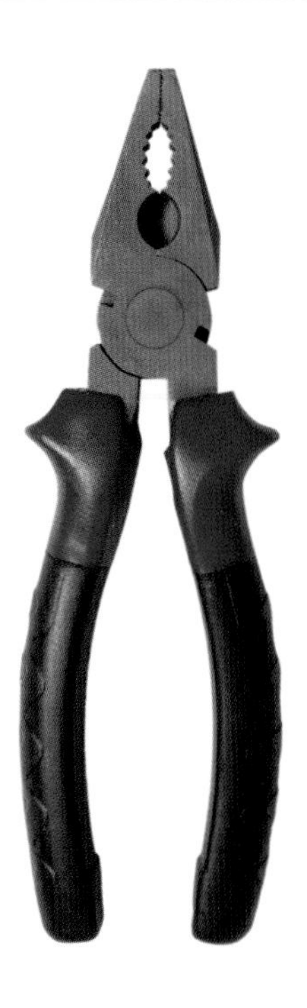

What to do:

1. Collect a selection of old or unused wood pieces with nails or screws left in them, alternatively unused/unwanted wooden furniture such as chairs, small tables.
2. Demonstrate for the children how to use pliers safely to pull the nails and screws out of the wood..
3. Encourage the children to use their bodily strengths.
4. Discuss the experience with the children, including the possible uses of pliers.

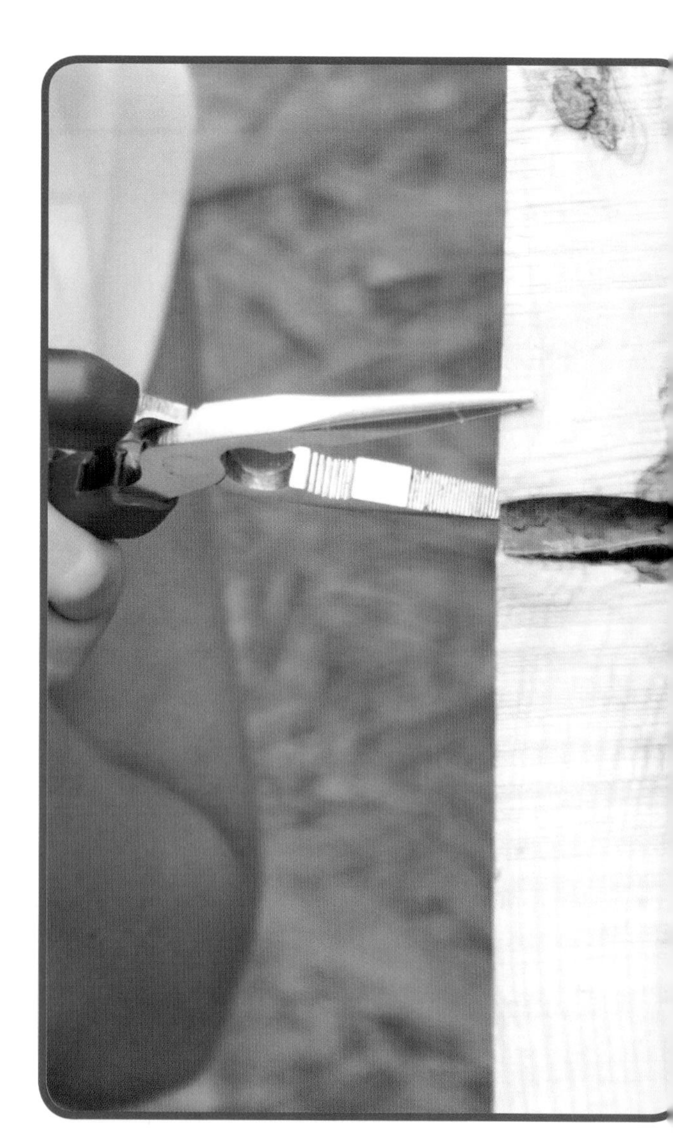

Taking it forward

- Use the demolished pieces and create something new, for example make a small box out of a chair.
- Use a selection of tools and create kindling and firewood.

What's in it for the children?

Children will gain a better understanding of recycling processes, the cycle of life and the human impact on the earth and its materials. They will therefore care for their environment more.

Observation question

- How well developed are the child's fine motor skills?

ud race

sk element: possibility of trips, falls, environmental factors such as weather

What you need:

- A large, naturally muddy area or a large sandpit
- Markers such as long bamboo sticks
- Timer

What to do:

1. Select a large natural area that becomes slightly muddy after rain. Alternatively wet the sand in a large sandpit.
2. Nominate a start and end point for the race and mark it clearly.
3. Ask the children to line up in pairs by the starting point. Get ready, get set and go! Start the race and time it. Encourage all the children to complete the race and congratulate them all.
4. If possible, encourage children to race barefoot.
5. Discuss the experience with the children: did their feet sink, what did their feet feel like etc.

king it forward

- Video the runners and replay the footage for the children as a discussion point.
- Organise a mud hopping race.

hat's in it for the children?

ildren will learn about the different nditions in their environment and erefore better understand the eather-associated risks.

bservation questions

- Can the children move confidently in a variety of conditions?
- Can the children understand the impact of movement on their body?

Health & Safety

Always thoroughly check the running area before the children begin to race, checking for any stones or other stray harmful objects.

Tightrope walking

Risk element: playing at a height

What you need:

- A long skipping rope, masking tape or a long tree branch

What to do:

1. Place the rope or masking tape in a straight line on the floor or ground, or find a natural place where children ca climb at an acceptable height on a long tree branch.
2. Invite the children to pretend they are walking the tightrope like an acrobat in the circus or as a superhero
3. Once the children are comfortable walking in a forward direction, invite them to walk sideways in both direction and, finally, backwards.
4. Later the height can be adjusted to challenge children further.

Taking it forward

- Make themed costumes and organise a tightrope balancing competition.
- Create a superhero story about a character whose power is tightrope walking and act the story out.
- Try placing toys or other objects like beanbags at a few points along the line for the children to hop or jump over them.
- A pool noodle makes an excellent stick to hold for help with balancing while crossing the tightrope.

What's in it for the children?

Children will gain different locomotor skills, and the different ways to move across the tightrope will develop their problem-solving abilities.

Observation question

- Do children use a variety of locomotor skills such as tiptoeing, galloping, hopping etc.?

Making a football pitch

Risk element: handling sharp or heavy tools

What you need:

- **A small area for the football pitch**
- **Shovels**
- **Rakes**
- **Grass seed**
- **Hand push cylinder** (non electric) **lawnmower**

What's in it for the children?

Children will develop self-esteem and confidence by completing the project. They will have a deeper understanding of the connection between human acts and processes, which will strengthen their sense of responsibility.

Observation questions

- Can the children show a sense of responsibility?
- Are the children interested in new activities?

What to do:

1. Find a plot for your football pitch.
2. If the pitch already does not have good quality grass, shovel the area. Demonstrate to the children how to use the shovels.
3. Make sure the children are wearing safe, strong shoes and ensure they do not get too tired or dehydrated.
4. Once ready (this is usually done in steps over a course of couple of days) ease the top of the soil with the shovels and rakes.
5. Finally sow the grass seeds and water regularly.
6. Alternatively, if the pitch has a good quality grass, mow the grass with a hand push cylinder lawnmower, after demonstrating for the children how to use it.
7. Operate very slowly; carry out the project in several steps.
8. Use the pitch for some team games.

Taking it forward

- Create a gardening plot.
- Carry out lawn mowing for charity in communal places such as playgrounds or parks.

Handling animals

Risk element: handling live animals

What you need:

- Pets from home
- Small animals such as bugs, creepy crawlies (woodlice, ladybirds, worms, grasshoppers) found in the wild

What to do:

1. Find a quiet open space for the children to sit in a semi-circle.
2. Ask the children to be calm and quiet.
3. Carefully and confidently handle an animal, taking it around for children to see in the first round.
4. Give the children the free choice to handle the animals, but never force them to do so.
5. Ask the children to hold their palm, the back of their hands or their forearm out for the animal to be placed on.
6. Go around and carefully place the animal on their hands/arms.
7. When observing/handling wild animals, do set them free as soon as possible and return pets to their owners or safety cages.

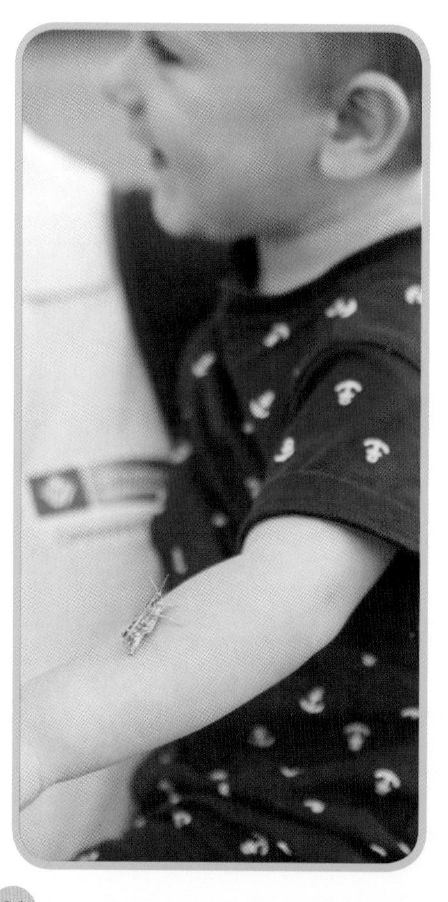

Taking it forward

- Nominate a keeper/helper.
- Encourage children to bring in their pets for a day.

What's in it for the children?

Children will develop a respect for non-human living beings and therefore learn to take better care of themselves and their environment. Through handling animals they will connect to them and understand their characteristics, lives and needs.

Observation questions

- Can the children overcome their fears (if any) when handling animals?
- Can the children understand the responsibility of handling living beings?

Health & Safety

Make sure children always wash their hands after handling creepy crawlies or small animals.

Cocktail making

Risk element: handling sharp, heavy, or electric equipment

What you need:

- Fresh coconut
- Corkscrew
- Drinking glass
- Plastic bag
- Hammer
- Knives, cutting board
- Fresh ginger
- Lemon
- Coriander
- Ginger drink
- Honey
- Ice cubes
- Small blender
- Sieve

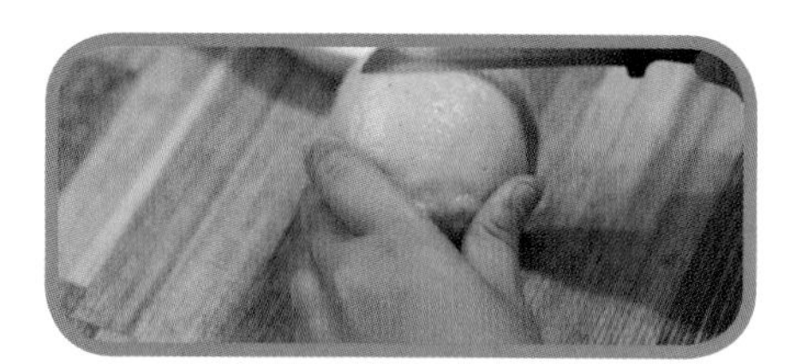

Taking it forward

- Make a selection of cocktails based on the children's choices of flavours and organise a cocktail party.
- Video the process to create a demonstration video.

What's in it for the children?

Children will be able to observe a production process from start to finish and be able to share their own produce. Their sharing ability, sense of community and observation skills will strengthen in the meantime.

Observation question

- Can the children operate tools and equipment sensibly?

What to do:

1. To open the coconut use the corkscrew to screw the coconut's eyes (three darker dots on one end). Put it over a glass and let the juice drain out. Put the coconut in a plastic bag and smash it with a hammer on the floor. Once cracked open, take some of the white flesh and dice finely.
2. Peel and dice ginger.
3. Cut up lemon into wedges, or cut it in half and squeeze to extract the juice.
4. Place coriander strings, lemon juice, coconut juice, coconut pieces, ginger pieces, ginger drink, honey and ice cubes into the electric blender and process until you have a fine sludge.
5. Sieve to extract the cocktail. Serve in cups for snack time.
6. The leftover pulp can be used in a biscuit dough.

Takeaway

Risk element: handling raw food, sharp tools, hot appliances

What you need:

- Cutting boards
- Knives
- Raw potatoes
- Colander
- A raw chicken breast
- Small portable electric hob
- Oil
- Selection of spices
- Frying pan
- Paper plates

What to do:

1. Instruct the children to clean their hands and explain why this is important.
2. Wash the potato thoroughly in a colander and cut it into small cubes. For smaller children cut the potato in half first, so they can lay it securely on the cutting board.
3. Using another board, cut the chicken into small strips.
4. Once all ingredients are cut, aid children in washing their hands again.
5. Set the electric hob safely on a table on the children's height, with the wire kept out of reach.
6. Place the cut up ingredients, oil and spices into a large frying pan and cook the food slowly.
7. Use paper plates to imitate a takeaway dinner.

Taking it forward

- Organise a charity picnic.
- Prepare raw fish and cook it.

What's in it for the children?

Children will develop a sense of responsibility and therefore act more focused and confident in their daily lives. They will gain an understanding of basic life experiences such as where food comes from, how food is prepared etc, which will grow their interest and knowledge of the world.

Observation questions

- Can the children follow instructions?
- Do the children act responsibly when given purpose?

Health & Safety

Make sure children understand that they must not lick their fingers or touch other surfaces after handling the raw chicken.

Dishwashing

Risk element: handling hot water, handling slippery objects

INDOOR PLAY

What you need:

- Large plastic bowls or cups
- Selection of sponges and cloths
- Dishwashing liquid
- Kitchen towel
- Rubber gloves

What to do:

1. Try this activity after cooking or snack time.
2. Fill the bowls with warm water.
3. Ask the children to be calm and quiet so as to avoid dropping objects.
4. Encourage the children to clean the bowls and cups using the dishwashing equipment.
5. Rinse the washed dishes well and place on a kitchen towel to dry.

Observation questions

- Can the children concentrate and follow instructions?
- Do the children display confidence when approaching new tasks?
- Do the children display muscle control when handling objects?

Taking it forward

- Wash cars to collect money for charity.
- Move the classroom's books and clean the bookshelves.

What's in it for the children?

Children's concentration and motor skills will develop via handling the small, slippery objects, and their sense of responsibility will also strengthen when given purposeful tasks to complete.

Jam making

Risk element: handling sharp equipment, electric equipment, hot appliances

INDOOR PLAY

What you need:

- 1kg strawberries
- 750g sugar (if possible, jam sugar)
- Knife
- Chopping board
- Potato masher or blender
- Wooden spoon
- Large saucepan
- Small portable electric hob
- Plate, chilled
- Clean jam jars

What to do:

1. Wash the strawberries thoroughly and chop them roughly with a paring knife on a chopping board.
2. Place the strawberries into the saucepan and crush with the masher (alternatively blend in a blender).
3. Set the electric hob safely on a table at the children's height, with the wire kept out of reach.
4. Add the sugar and heat gently, stirring with a wooden spoon until all the sugar has dissolved.
5. Bring it to the boil and time for five minutes, stirring occasionally.
6. Test a drop of jam on a chilled plate and place in the fridge for 30 seconds.
7. If set and slightly cooled, empty the jam into glass jars.

Taking it forward

- Serve the jam at an afternoon tea event, and allow children to slice and butter their own bread.
- Make jam for charity or for a harvest giveaway.

What's in it for the children?

Children will be able to test themselves in slightly risky activities, and pushing their own limits will give them satisfaction and grow their confidence.

Observation question

- Can the children handle dangerous items responsibility, following rules and instructions?

Health & Safety

- Make sure you closely supervise the children as they stir the jam. The jam will be extremely hot, and because it's sticky it can cause bad burns.
- Fill the jam jars yourself and make sure children stand back from the hot jam, or closely supervise more capable older children.

Smoothie making

Risk element: handling sharp electric equipment

What you need:

- Selection of fruit such as bananas, strawberries, raspberries, blueberries etc.
- Fresh herbs such as mint and lemongrass (optional)
- Knife
- Chopping board
- Blender

What to do:

1. Remind the children to wash their hands.
2. Wash, peel and dry the fruit.
3. Wash the herbs if used.
4. Place the fruit in a blender and securely place the lid on before operating.
5. Make the smoothie and serve in chilled glasses for snack time.

Taking it forward

- Make a simple ice cream by blending banana and berries and then freezing the mixture.
- Process a mixture of roasted seeds to create a unique food topping.

What's in it for the children?

Children will develop greater confidence when being given responsibility and being trusted to use adult equipment.

Observation questions

- Can the children understand basic processes such as making food in order to eat?
- Are the children confident when having to handle equipment?

ꟻish-dish

꞉sk element: handling raw food, sharp tools, hot appliances

INDOOR PLAY

What you need:

- A raw fish (gutted), - a species that has large scales is best
- Colander
- Knives: a butter knife or scaling tool and a sharper knife suitable for filleting
- Large wooden kitchen board board
- Frying pan
- Cooking oil and a selection of spices
- Small portable electric hob
- Paper plates and paper kitchen towels

What to do:

1. Instruct the children to wash their hands and explain why it is important before handling food.
2. Wash the fish thoroughly in a colander and place on a large wooden kitchen board.
3. Begin scaling the fish: hold it firmly and scrape the scales from the tail toward the gills. Use a butter knife or a scaling tool. Test for the right pressure – the scales should come off easily. Keep the strokes short and quick.
4. To obtain a fillet: with a sharper knife, blade pointing away from the person and across the body of the fish, begin to cut toward the head. Use the backbone to guide the knife. Take the skin off - begin by holding the fillet by the tail, skin side down. Cut the fillet into manageable strips.
5. Set the electric hob safely on a table at the children's height, with the wire kept out of reach.
6. Place the cut-up fish, oil and spices into a large frying pan and cook the food slowly.
7. Use paper plates and paper kitchen towels to drain excess oil.

king it forward

Prepare and cook raw chicken.

Make a fish soup.

hat's in it for the children?

ıildren may learn about the value their abilities and their personal ꞉hievement by being able to ▪mplete more difficult tasks.

ɔservation questions

Can the children work carefully?

Do the children understand the risk of the activity (to an age-appropriate extent)?

Pancake frying

Risk element: handling hot substances and hot equipment

What you need:

- To make the pancake mix:
  - · 100g plain flour
  - · 2 eggs
  - · 300ml milk
  - · 1 tbsp oil
  - · a pinch of salt
- Oil
- Frying pans
- Spatula, ladle
- Portable electric hob

What to do:

1. Instruct the children to wash their hands and explain why this is important.
2. Prepare the pancake batter by mixing all the ingredients together. Set the electric hob safely on a table at the children's height, with the wire kept out of reach.
3. Place the frying pan with a spoonful of oil on the hob and heat.
4. Aid the children to pour one ladleful of pancake batter into the frying pan. Make sure there is a safe distance between the children and the heated, sizzling oil.
5. Aid the children when turning the pancake with a spatula. Also help them to remove the pancake from the pan.

Taking it forward

- Make spicy pancakes by adding cinnamon, nutmeg, ground ginger or orange zest to the pancake batter.
- Make American pancakes as a variation.

What's in it for the children?

Children will learn about health and safety requirements within their own environment. They will understand how to control themselves and be careful in a situation where there is greater than normal risk and can potentially be hazardous.

Observation questions

- Do the children approach the task without fear?
- Do the children show developed self-control?

Making pesto

Risk element: handling heavy tools

What you need:

- Fresh herbs
- Oil
- Pine nuts
- Salt
- Pestle and mortar
- Electric grinder, optional

What to do:

1. Instruct the children to wash their hands and explain why it is important to do this before handling food.
2. Place the herbs, oil, salt and pine nuts into the mortar.
3. For smoother results, children may grind the ingredients in an electric grinder first (or they can have a go with the pestle and mortar first, and use the grinder to refine the consistency).
4. Pound or bash the ingredients in the mortar with the pestle.
5. To avoid mishaps, cup the nonworking hand or a small cloth over the top of the mortar to catch any of the bashed items that may bounce out.
6. Bash for as long as possible, letting the children take turns for the best results.
7. Place the pesto into a glass jar for storage. Use on freshly cooked pasta or roast meat.

Taking it forward

- Make a spice blend using the pestle and mortar.

What's in it for the children?

Children will develop physical strength and a more advanced sense of control over their own power.

Observation questions

- Can the children control and direct their own efforts?
- Do the children understand the impact of their own physical strength?

ʻnack duty

ʻsk element: handling sharp tools

INDOOR PLAY

What you need:

- Cutting board
- Non-stick mat
- A selection of bread rolls
- Butter
- Bread and butter knives
- Various snack vegetables

What to do:

1. Make sure that everyone has had a snack before starting the cooking project. If they are starving, they are likely to rush.
2. Instruct the children to wash their hands and explain why it is important to do this before handling food.
3. Place the cutting board on a non-stick mat on a straight, clear surface.
4. Demonstrate for the children how to cut the rolls and butter the bread.
5. Encourage the children to cut slowly and apply controlled pressure.
6. Aid children during the process to achieve individual success.
7. When cutting vegetables, make sure that they are washed thoroughly first.
8. Enjoy the freshly cut vegetables and buttered rolls.

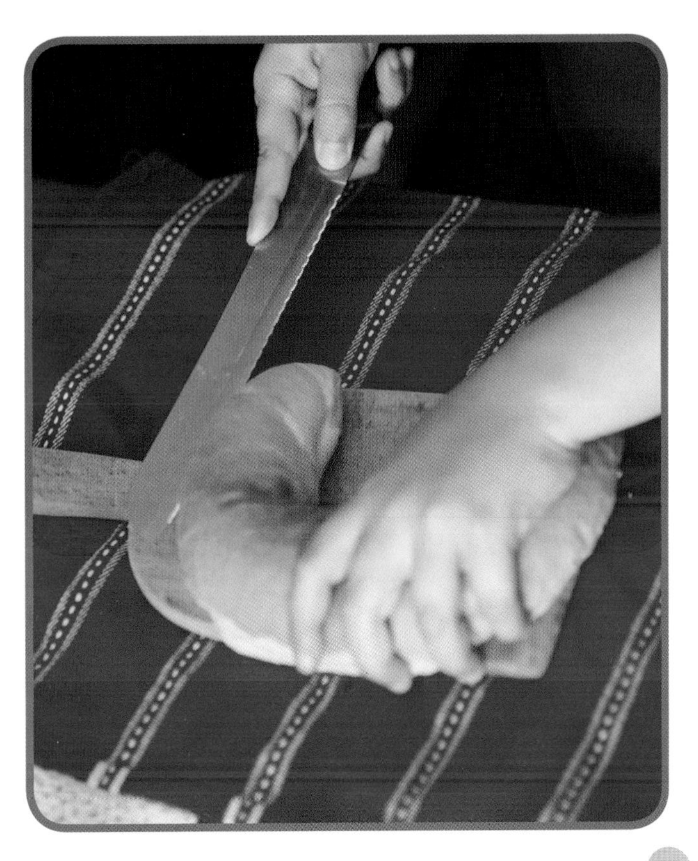

king it forward

Dice bread slices and toss them in flavoured oil to bake croutons.

Cut vegetables to make a salad.

hat's in it for the children?

ɜxt to the important developments fine motor skills, muscle control and ʼengthening concentration, children ɫl also learn to take responsibility ıilst being able to demonstrate ɺlependence.

ɔservation questions

Do the children approach the task without fear?

Do the children show developed self-control?

Puzzle making

Risk element: handling sharp tools

What you need:

- Marker pens or crayons
- Card in various colours or thin cardboard
- Old magazines
- Scissors
- Glue
- X-Acto knife

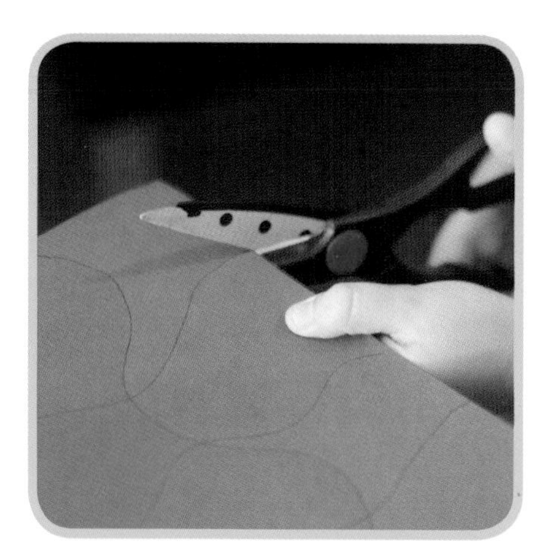

What to do:

1. Help children to decide if they want to cut a picture fro a magazine or draw their own pictures.
2. Hand them the markers or crayons if they are drawing their own design.
3. If they would rather choose a picture from a magazine, let them cut it out, then help them glue the picture to the card or cardboard. Leave it to dry. When the glue is completely dry, use the scissors to trim the cardboard/ card to fit the picture exactly.
4. With older children use an X-Acto knife to cut the pictu on the cardboard into squiggly shapes. The smaller the pieces, the more challenging the puzzle will be.
5. Small children should use thinner card that they are ab to cut into pieces themselves.
6. Make sure children hold the scissors correctly before they start to apply pressure.
7. When finished, cut each picture into pieces, mix them up and give each puzzle to another child to solve.

Taking it forward

- Make photo puzzles as presents.
- Make large floor puzzle with a group of children.

What's in it for the children?

Children will gain fine motor control and develop physical skills. They will also have a strengthened independence via succeeding in difficult, potentially dangerous tasks, and therefore have greater confidence.

Observation questions

- Do the children show interest even when aware of risks?
- Can the children understand their own success?

roning

isk element: handling hot equipment

INDOOR PLAY

What you need:

- A sturdy table at the children's height
- A heatproof cover for the table, such as large, thick sheets
- A well-working, undamaged iron
- Items to iron such as: napkins, tea towels, baby vests, muslins etc.

What to do:

1. This task should only be undertaken by children who have practised responsible tasks before.
2. Instruct the children to work slowly with this task and explain why it is important that they do so.
3. Show the children how to turn the iron on and stress how hot it is once it is plugged in.
4. Talk to them about keeping the iron moving so that clothes are not burned.
5. When teaching children how to do something new, it's important NOT to overwhelm them.
6. With this task teach them one or two parts at a time and let them get comfortable with the task, then show them something new.

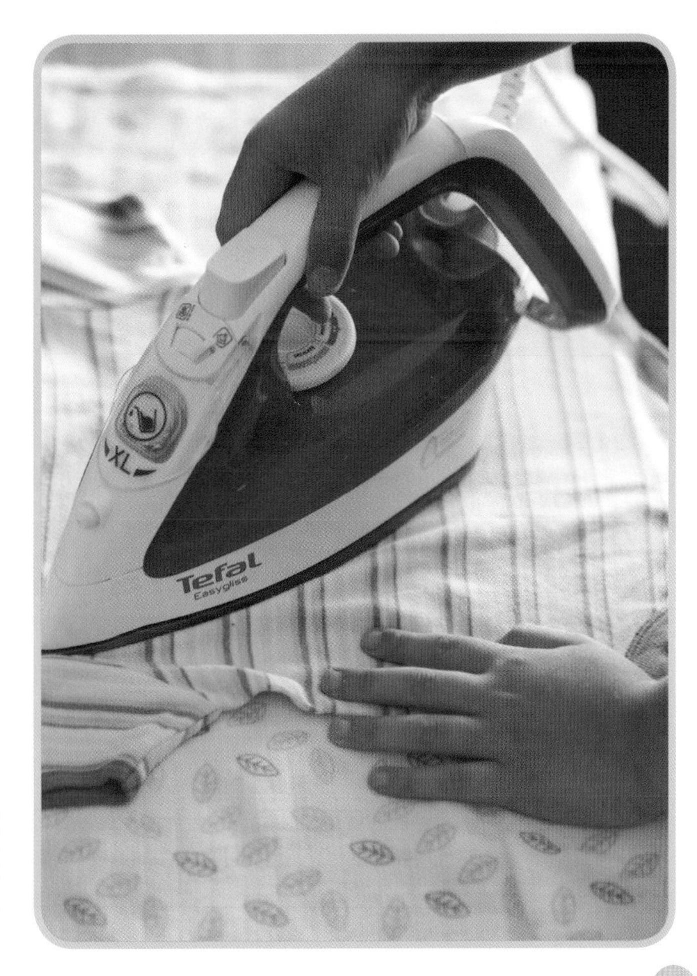

king it forward

Try/explore the old-fashioned iron heated with live coals.

hat's in it for the children?

ɔt only will the children learn how do everyday tasks, it will also help əm to become more self-reliant, more ıpowered and more knowledgeable out how to take care of themselves.

ɔservation questions

Do the children approach the task without fear?

Do the children show developed self-control?

Health & Safety

Demonstrate to the children how to hold the iron, and make sure they know to always rest the iron upright when it is not in use.

Hairdresser role-play

Risk element: handling hot equipment

What you need:

- Hairdryers with protective air concentrator
- No-tangle hairbrushes with longer handles
- Simple hair curlers such as the soft foam variety
- Spray bottle filled with water
- Hairstyle magazines

What to do:

1. Explain to the children what they will need to do and talk about visits they may have made to a hairdresser.
2. Demonstrate how to turn the hairdryer on and highlight how hot it will be once it is on.
3. Stress the importance of keeping a safe distance between the head and the equipment and of keeping the dryer moving.
4. Encourage the children to take roles in turns.
5. Spray the 'customer' child's hair with water and use rollers to hold styles.
6. Encourage the children to chose and create hairstyles and then dry the hair.
7. Take photos of the children's creations and make a catalogue.

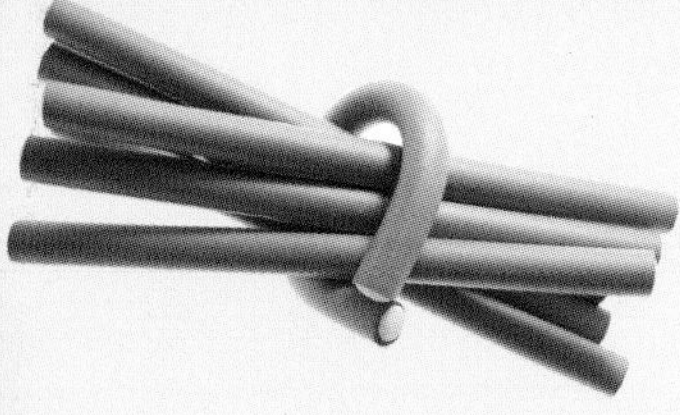

ɑking it forward

- Use a variation of hair styling tools such as curlers or hairdryer with a diffuser etc.
- Organise a hair stylist competition.

/hat's in it for the children?

ʰhildren will experience feelings ssociated with purposeful activities uch as the joy of helping others and ıe pride of personal success.

ʰbservation questions

- Are the children aware of risks within everyday tasks?
- Do the children enjoy taking pride in their appearance?

Woodwork

Risk element: handling sharp tools

What you need:

- Small handsaw
- Safety gloves
- Variety of log offcuts, wood pieces and driftwood
- Workbench or vice

Taking it forward

- Carry out projects that need simple sawing such as jigsaw puzzles, talking stick, tripod for camera etc.
- Visualise a fantasy story with the cut-off wood pieces as characters.

What's in it for the children?

Young children love the idea of handling real tools, and through focused teaching they can gain a basic knowledge about what tools are used for what purposes, and how they are used.

Observation questions

- Do the children handle risky activities with care?

What to do:

1. Instruct the children how to operate the saw and point out the sharp parts. Make sure the children wear a strong safety glove on their non-working hand.
2. Secure the wood to a workbench or a vice. Leave plen of space to work around the wood.
3. Mark the line to be cut.
4. Place the handsaw on top of the wood, slightly away from where the cut line was drawn.
5. Grip the handle of the saw.
6. The hand that is not holding the saw should rest on the piece of wood in order to keep it still and secure.
7. Start the cut without applying pressure onto the saw and pull back.
8. Start applying pressure.
9. Continue the sawing motion until the piece of wood is ready to break off.
10. Slow down and apply less force towards the end, to avoid cracking or splintering the wood.
11. Hold on to the piece that is cut off to prevent the weigh of the wood from breaking it.

Hammering nails

Risk element: handling heavy tools and sharp objects

INDOOR PLAY

What you need:

- Wood pieces
- Workbench or table
- Nails in various sizes
- Hammer with shorter, strong handle

What to do:

1. Instruct the children to work slowly and listen to the rules.
2. Encourage the children to observe their material and make a plan about what they are about to make.
3. Place the wood pieces securely on the workbench or table.
4. For a first attempt at hammering down nails the adult should insert the nail into the wood and hammer it half-way in. This means the child won't need to hold onto the nail for support, so helps to avoid any injuries caused by doing this.
5. Children should first be encouraged to practise the hammering movement without force or pressure.
6. The child can then be allowed to hammer the rest of the nail in.

Taking it forward

- Mend broken, damaged furniture with the children.
- Earn 'woodworking licences' by completing simple tasks such as hammering a nail in independently, sawing a stick, sanding a piece of wood etc.

What's in it for the children?

Children will develop hand-eye co-ordination, learn manual skills, grow self-confidence, find expression for their natural creativity, develop problem-solving skills, build muscle strength, increase dexterity with their hands.

Observation questions

- Do the children approach the task without fear?
- Do the children show developed self-control?

Health & Safety

Monitor children closely while handling heavy or sharp objects, and be vigilant in checking for stray nails left around the setting.

Wreath making

Risk element: handling hot substances and equipment

What you need:

- **Sheet of paper, aluminium foil**
- **Low heat glue gun and glue stick**
- **Cardboard circle**
- **Various natural objects such as wood pieces, bark pieces, pebbles, shells, pine cones, dry plant pieces and dry crops** (acorn, cornhusk etc.)
- **Ribbon** (optional)

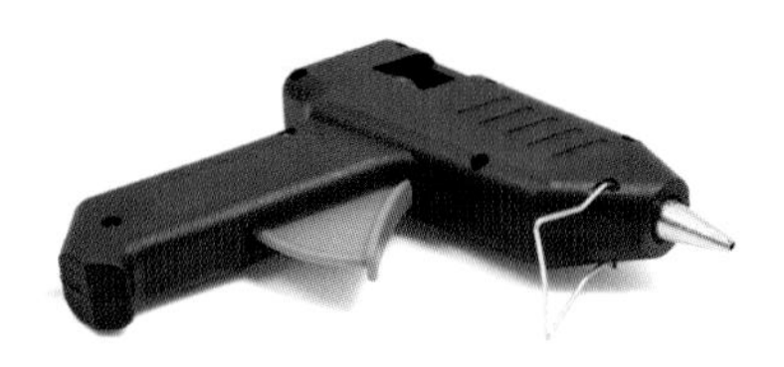

Taking it forward

- Make glue gun art by scribbling with the tip of the glue gun on black card, sprinkling over with glitter and tapping off the excess.
- Create a treasure montage on a cardboard piece by gluing on natural objects collected on a trip.

What's in it for the children?

Children will learn about health and safety requirements within their own environment. They will understand how to control themselves and be careful.

Observation questions

- Are the children able to control their movements?
- Can the children use self-control in order to succeed?

What to do:

1. Inspect the glue gun for cracks in the handle and body. Make sure there isn't any old glue clogging the nozzle. If damaged do not use it!
2. Take the plug and insert it into an electrical outlet or wall socket. That step should be done by an adult.
3. Place the glue gun on a secure surface such as a table. Place a sheet of paper underneath it to protect the surface area. Place a piece of aluminium foil under the nozzle of the glue gun to catch the over-flow of glue that will run out of the nozzle. Be sure to keep the glue gun away from open flames.
4. Insert a glue stick into the back of the glue gun. If there is already a glue stick in the glue gun, wait until the glue gun warms up and then gently squeeze the trigger.
5. Once the glue gun has been plugged in for a few minutes, gently squeeze the trigger to see if the glue is hot enough to flow out of the nozzle.
6. Have all of your materials ready when starting a project. Lay down the cardboard circle to act as a guide in making an aesthetical circular shape.
7. Put a small amount of glue on the back of each piece, place them in their desired place and press firmly.
8. If desired, lead a ribbon through the wreath and tie for a wall hanger.

ewing

sk element: handling sharp tools

INDOOR PLAY

What you need:

- Pieces of cardboard
- Mesh from fruit or veg (e.g. a bag of oranges)
- Stapler
- Scissors
- X-Acto knife
- Needles (embroidery needle with blunt tip)
- Thick embroidery yarn in various colours
- Fabric pieces

What to do:

1. Gather appropriate materials to help young children to get the hang of stitching and sewing first.
2. Cut the cardboard and mesh. The mesh will essentially be used as a sewing surface, and the cardboard is used to stabilise the mesh as a frame (like the cross-stitch frame and fabric). Cut the cardboard and mesh any size that is suitable for the children to manipulate.
3. Attach the mesh to the cardboard using the stapler with the mesh being longer and wider than the cardboard frame, so you can pull the mesh taught over the cardboard and it is not too flexible in the frame.
4. Thread the needle and then show the children how to stitch in and out of the mesh squares. Change the colour of the thread (or yarn) to create a more exciting look, allow the children to chose and name the colours.
5. Once you have shown them how to stitch, let the children have a go at it however they want. Don't worry about 'normal' sewing rules just let them experiment with stitches and colours.
6. After some practice, cut two pieces of fabric squares each and encourage the children to stitch them together.

aking it forward

- Use a marker to draw patterns for the children to follow.
- Sew the children's stitched fabric pieces together to make a large blanket, floor mat or tablecloth.

/hat's in it for the children?

hildren will follow instructions to learn new skill, developing manual dexterity s they practice.

bservation questions

- Do the children demonstrate developed muscle control? Can they handle small tools?
- Can the children work together to create something as a group?

Tunnel building

Risk element: handling sharp tools and objects

What you need:

- Paper, pencil
- Long, bendy sticks
- Small secateurs
- Safety gloves
- Shovel
- Willow or other living sticks
- Raffia

What to do:

1. Encourage the children to draw a plan of their fence or stick structure.
2. Try to estimate the length of sticks needed for the structure.
3. Demonstrate for the children how to use the secateurs.
4. Encourage the children to wear a glove on their non-working hand.
5. Make sure children hold the secateurs firmly and confidently before applying pressure.
6. Cut the sticks carefully with secateurs.
7. To make the structure: mark out two trenches, dig to a depth of 30 cm and mix with compost. Insert two poles opposite each other along the length of the trenches at a spacing of approximately 25 cm. Bend each pair of poles together to form an arch and tie the end of each pole wi raffia pieces. To increase the stability of the structure, secure a pole along the length of the tunnel at the apex curves. In order to build up the sides of the tunnel insert woven poles at an angle of approximately 45 degrees at the base of each side. Shorter poles can be used towarc the rear of the tunnel to enhance the tapering effect.

aking it forward

Make an artistic woven fence by weaving ribbons and long colourful fabric pieces into the structure.

hat's in it for the children?

hildren will learn about doing ings for themselves, providing a ngstanding natural attraction for their wn play, they also learn responsibility, ride and independence.

bservation questions

Do the children enjoy a new challenge?

Do the children stay focused for longer periods of time?

Weight-lifting

Risk element: handling own physical power, heavy objects

INDOOR PLAY

What you need:

- **A selection of bags** (plastic bag, paper bag, reusable fabric bag)
- **A selection of dry, wrapped food items** (such as flour, sugar, cans, dry beans, rice etc.)

What to do:

1. Lay the food items on a table.
2. Hand the children a bag of their choice and then ask them to estimate how much they could carry and pack the items in their bag.
3. Appoint a route and a destination table and then encourage the children to carry their bags around.
4. Challenge them to pack each others' bags.
5. Discuss the experience, including asking how did their body feel, how can they become stronger, why is it important to be strong etc.

Taking it forward

- Try weight lifting with small training weights.

What's in it for the children?

Children will learn about using their own skills to be helpful, whilst also gaining knowledge about how to take care of themselves when completing tasks.

Observation questions

- Can the children understand their own limits?
- Can the children make guesses about their peers? Do children look after their peers when in a risky situation?

ndoor skateboard run

isk element: engaging in possibly dangerous sport

What you need:

- **A long piece of old rug** (store offcuts or showroom pieces)
- **Skateboards**

aking it forward

Organise a short skateboard-run competition during sports day.

/hat's in it for the children?

lore than just a means to move ɔ places, riding a skateboard is a trength-building activity as it requires alance, bravery, leg power and tamina. By learning to skateboard hildren will understand the need to ake the time to practise things properly, oth for joy and safety. It promotes a ealthy, outdoor lifestyle, and teaches hildren about approaching danger with nowledge and caution.

bservation questions

How do children behave when they know they could get hurt?

Do the children display courage when encountering unknown situations?

What to do:

1. To prepare the area: situate the rug in a flat, clear area (where children cannot fall near furniture).
2. Place a skateboard on the rug with the wheels on the ground. This reduces the movement of the board.
3. Step, stand and jump on the board to get used to the platform.
4. Practise balancing on the board with the dominant foot (the foot children kick a ball with) to the back and the front foot planted. Bend knees with shoulders facing forward.
5. Push the body forward with the back foot while balancing on the front foot. You will need to practise balancing and this may feel awkward at first.
6. Push forward until there is enough momentum to roll a little bit.
7. Bring your rear foot back on the board as you roll, using bent knees and your arms to aid body balance.
8. Stop by putting the back foot on the ground.

Get lost!

Risk element: handling unknown spaces

What you need:

- A map of the rooms in the building/a professional floor map
- Room monitors for each area of the building

What's in it for the children?

Children will learn how to approach freedom and why it is important to listen to instructions and keep to rules even when being free.

Observation question

- Do the children use their initiative to find their way in unknown situations?

What to do:

1. Tell the children the rules of freely accessing all of the rooms in the building, except facility rooms such as the sluice room, laundry room, adult bathrooms, staff rooms and kitchen.
2. Before starting the activity, make sure there are appointed adults within each accessible area (even in corridors) to minimise risk such as younger children accessing toys which are not age-appropriate.
3. Encourage children to visit as many parts of the site as possible.
4. Prepare a map of the building together with the children.

Taking it forward

- Organise a treasure hunt.
- Act out stories that involve walking around such as 'We are going on a bear hunt'.

orch-lit tag

isk element: handling unknown spaces, playing outside comfort zone

INDOOR PLAY

What you need:

- Torches
- Dark sheet or dark fabric to blind the windows/doors

What to do:

1. Explain the rules to the children: like the original version of tag, the game is to evade the tag of the player who is designated 'it'.
2. Darken the room as being tagged in this game means getting lit up by a torch.
3. The game begins with a hide-and-seek element: one player selected as 'it' counts to a pre determined number while the rest of the players hide. Armed with only a torch, 'it' heads into the dark in search of the hidden players. Players are tagged when the torch beams on them, at which point they become 'it' or are simply out until the rest of the players are found.

aking it forward

- Organise dark room storytelling.
- Create a space on the ceiling from luminous paper and observe the stars.

hat's in it for the children?

hildren will learn to overcome their ars and realise how some common eliefs can be misconceptions. hough the exercise they will gain onfidence and self-respect.

bservation questions

- Do the children overcome fear?
- How do the children approach new, unusual situations?

Box tunnel

Risk element: handling sharp tools, handling unknown spaces (dark tunnel)

What you need:

- Cardboard boxes in various sizes
- X-Acto knifes
- Scissors
- Duct tape/double-sided tape or glue

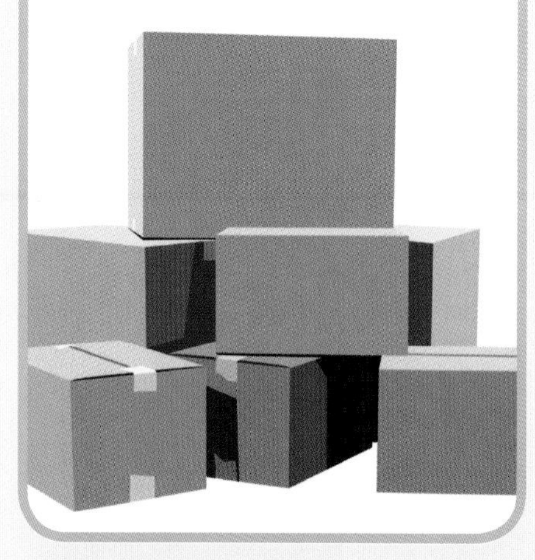

What to do:

1. Provide a selection of cardboard boxes for the children and ask them to plan a tunnel they would like to build. It might be helpful to decide what size and shape you want the holes to be beforehand and create a template.
2. Gather/select some boxes. It is important that the boxes all be about the same size, or at least that they fit together end-to-end with no big gaps in between the boxes. The project will probably need at least five boxes, depending on their size and the amount of space given to build the tunnel.
3. Design the tunnel. Put the boxes together and decide where to cut the holes, cutting only on some sides so that the children are led towards the end of the tunnel.
4. Cut holes in the boxes. Once you have designed your maze, start cutting holes in the boxes with scissors or an X-Acto/utility knife. Make sure the holes are big enough for the children to fit through without getting stuck or feeling restricted.
5. Once you have cut holes in all the boxes, put the boxes together. Use glue or double-sided tape to stick the sides of each box together. Tape together the top edge of the boxes for added security.

ɪking it forward

Darken the room for added excitement when the tunnel is in use.

ɪhat's in it for the children?

ɪhildren will learn about how to ɪproach their environment in a variety ʼ ways and how to accept new, ɪallenging situations. With this activity ɪildren gain confidence and the bravery ill grow.

bservation questions

Can the children listen to instructions when handling tools?

Do they display a healthy confidence when approaching new situations?

Vacuum cleaning

Risk element: handling hot equipment

What you need:

- A vacuum cleaner

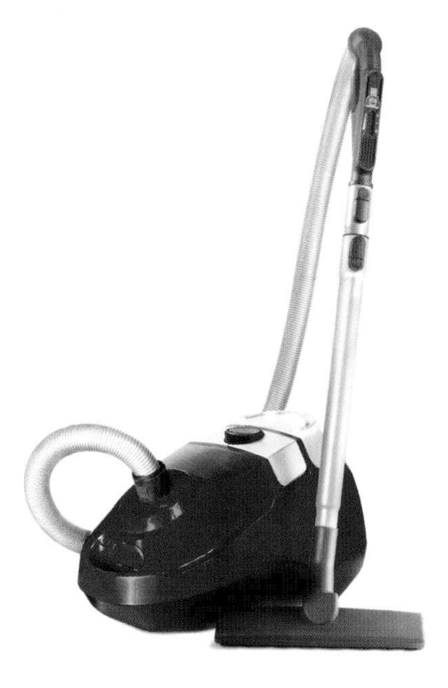

What to do:

1. Instruct the children to work slowly with this task and explain why it is important.
2. Show the children how to turn the vacuum cleaner on and stress how strong the suction is once it is plugged i
3. Talk to them about how to move the machine so it does not catch any unwanted objects.
4. Let all the children have a turn.
5. Talk about the experience, including how machines have electric power and how they need to approach it t minimise its risks.
6. Teach them how to switch it off and pack it away carefull

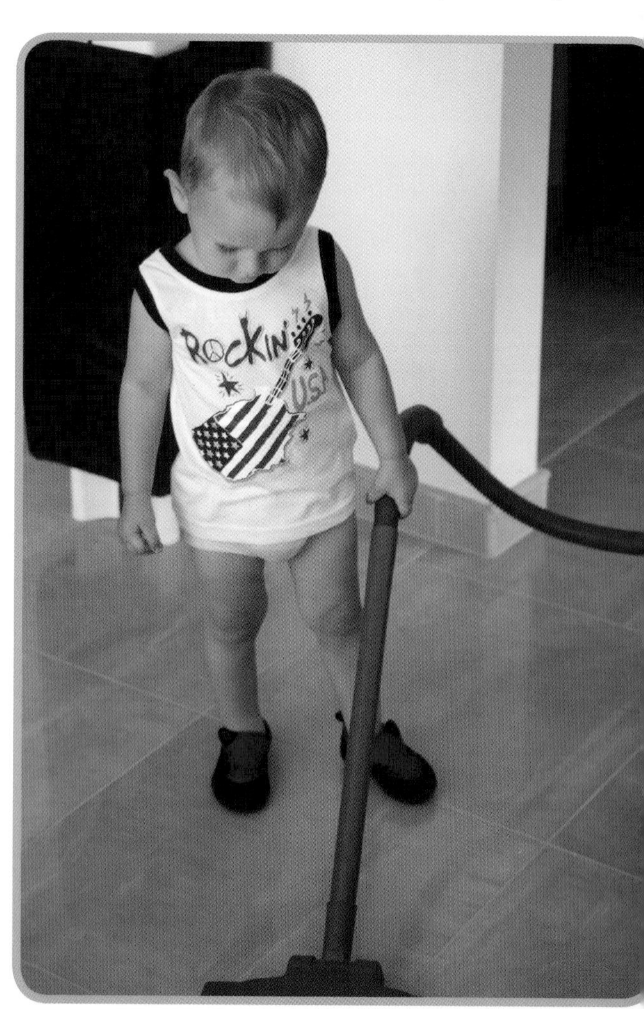

Taking it forward

- Explore other electric household items.

What's in it for the children?

The children learn how to approach and complete everyday tasks, feeling able and empowered, therefore growing in confidence.

Observation questions

- Do the children act responsibly with electrical equipment?

ʼindow cleaning

isk element: working on height

INDOOR PLAY

What you need:

- Small indoor stepladder
- Safety mats
- Fabric pieces
- Soapy water in a spray bottle

What to do:

1. Instruct the children about working at a height, stress the importance of always standing on both feet, always holding on the ladder with one hand and not to overstretch the width of the ladder.
2. When working with younger children, place safety mats around the ladder.
3. Make children take turns one-by-one. Encourage them to support their friends by holding onto the sides of the ladder.
4. When climbing the ladder grab onto the rungs of the ladder using a hand over hand method, never letting go of one rung before grabbing the next.
5. Make sure children have appropriate footwear.
6. Spray the window lightly in advance so children can easily clean the surface with the fabric pieces.
7. Make sure there is constant adult supervision.
8. Instruct them how to come back down the ladder placing a foot on the rungs in turn slowly to avoid slipping.

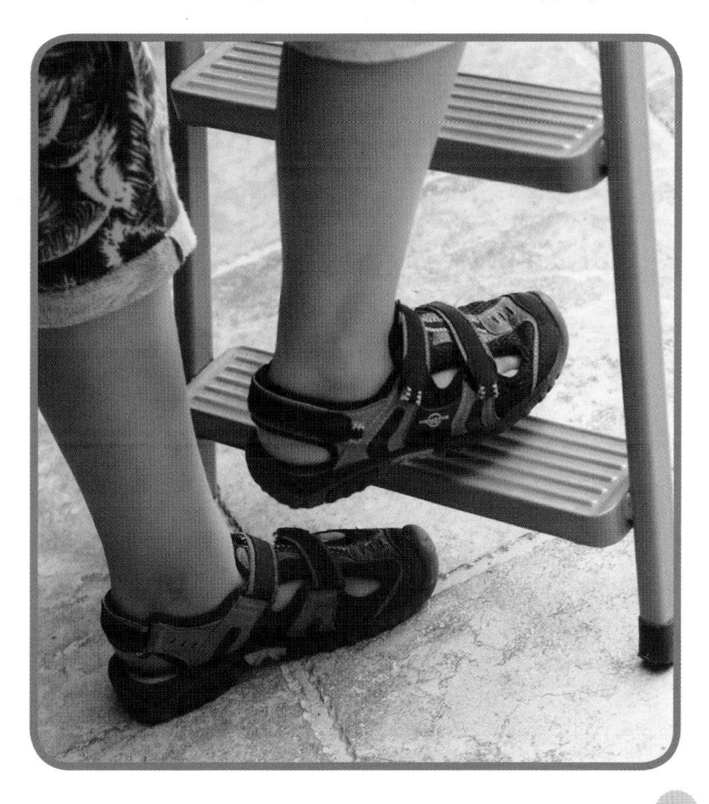

ıking it forward

Use ladders for a variety of purposeful tasks such as picking fruit, dusting furniture.

ʼhat's in it for the children?

imbing heights can be a wonderful ҁperience for a child, providing it is ɔne in a safe and supervised manner. ɔproaching heights boosts children's ɪlf-esteem, develops their balance and eir physical strengths. When used for purpose, this activity will aid children feeling appreciated and helpful.

bservation questions

Do the children display a brave attitude?

Do the children feel comfortable but responsible with potentially risky activities?

Hanging pictures

Risk element: working on height

What you need:

- Work platform
- Children's pictures
- Sticky tack

What to do:

1. Instruct the children about the task in advance; inform them about the purpose of the activity.
2. Use a work platform that is sturdy, undamaged and fits the children's height (low enough for the children to easily step up on it).
3. For younger children place safety mats around the work platform.
4. Demonstrate the right way to climb.
5. Whilst climbing/being on the platform, stress the importance of standing on both feet.
6. Prepare small amount of sticky tack to hand to children when securing wall decorations.
7. Determine the height at which to hang the pictures on, so as to ensure the children stay safe.

Taking it forward

- Use the working platform to clean shelves.

What's in it for the children?

Children perceive being up high as fun and strive to accomplish reaching the highest point possible, overcome challenges and testing their abilities. Being up high can build confidence and develop coordination, problem-solving skills, and strength, so children should be encouraged to climb heights safely. Children have a natural instinct to be cautious of heights, so when climbing they will learn skills to stabilise themselves and determine the best route to take.

Observation questions

- Are the children physically confident?